More Common Sense

A Fundamental Commentary on Personnel Management Subjects for Associations

Mark Frels

authorHOUSE

AuthorHouse™
1663 Liberty Drive
Bloomington, IN 47403
www.authorhouse.com
Phone: 1 (800) 839-8640

© 2017 Mark Frels. All rights reserved.

No part of this book may be reproduced, stored in a retrieval system, or transmitted by any means without the written permission of the author.

Published by AuthorHouse   08/08/2017

ISBN: 978-1-5462-0119-9 (sc)
ISBN: 978-1-5462-0117-5 (hc)
ISBN: 978-1-5462-0118-2 (e)

Library of Congress Control Number: 2017911933

Print information available on the last page.

Any people depicted in stock imagery provided by Thinkstock are models, and such images are being used for illustrative purposes only. Certain stock imagery © Thinkstock.

This book is printed on acid-free paper.

Because of the dynamic nature of the Internet, any web addresses or links contained in this book may have changed since publication and may no longer be valid. The views expressed in this work are solely those of the author and do not necessarily reflect the views of the publisher, and the publisher hereby disclaims any responsibility for them.

To the very dedicated members, leaders, staff, and employees of the county Farm Bureaus in Illinois and the Illinois Agricultural Association (Illinois Farm Bureau) and its affiliated companies.

Contents

About the Book ix

Chapter 1   Dealing with Candidates for Positions 1

Chapter 2   Interviewing Procedures 11

Chapter 3   Starting the New Job 27

Chapter 4   The Purposes and Mechanics
            of Performance Reviews 35

Chapter 5   The Individual Development Plan:
            Your Road Map 45

Chapter 6   Employee Performance Problems
            and Terminations 52

Chapter 7   Evaluating Attitude 63

Chapter 8   Analyzing Yourself as a Supervisor 72

Chapter 9   The Nature of Human Nature 76

Chapter 10 Author's Summary 97

About the Author 99

About the Book

This book provides fundamental opinions and commentary regarding commonsense and practical approaches to a wide variety of personnel and human-resources subjects from an association-management perspective.

This book is a companion to the author's first publication, *Just Common Sense ... a fundamental commentary on association management*.

The subjects included are intended to promote awareness, provide basic procedural information, and remind us of important factors as we go through our daily lives and careers.

It is the intent that the reader will take from this book ideas and procedures to manage these issues effectively and fairly.

Chapter 1

Dealing with Candidates for Positions

Most companies or associations use a standard two-pronged approach to surfacing candidates to fill positions. It is not rocket science. The company posts the position *in house*—meaning it posts the position to the existing employee pool—or the company posts the position to the outside world via various online job boards and newspapers.

Most associations or companies have an internal job-posting procedure managed by the human resources department. When it comes to posting a position outside the company, there are lots of electronic options available. Some companies still place an ad in the newspaper, which I realize is considered antiquated, but this happens and still can be effective. Almost all companies today, with few exceptions, have their own website with an employment section. These sites provide employment information and application procedures for open positions. The website should also provide information regarding the company itself, which is beneficial to existing and potential employees.

One of the challenges that comes with first posting a position to the outside and not posting internally can be dealing with the morale of existing employees. Obviously, if there are no qualified existing employees, then those challenges regarding the company "going outside" to hire someone should be minimal. However, employee morale will be much higher if the internal posting process is considered first if there could be existing employees who qualify to fill the position. This is true, especially if the position is considered a promotion position. Of course, this is not typically the case with entry-level positions.

Put yourself in the position of existing employees, especially those who consider themselves qualified for the posted position. Should the position be posted internally and no acceptable candidate surfaces, then the company should proceed to post the job to the outside world. However, from an employee morale and motivation standpoint, there is real value for the company to look internally first at the existing employee pool, to see if qualified candidates are available. I believe most companies already do this—or at least I hope they do.

When an internal employee is promoted (if viable), it provides a great lift and motivation for that employee, of course, but also for the overall employee population. This action sends a clear message from upper management that they have confidence in the current employees and consider them extremely valuable. The most valuable assets of any association or company are its leaders and employees. Of course, as always, when there is competition between existing employees for a promotion position, there will be disappointed employees. In my experience, even employees who went through the interview process but did not successfully secure the position usually (not always) later have some appreciation for the fact that they were part of the interview process and considered prior to outside candidates.

The amazing technology of today's world makes surfacing outside candidates a global activity and process. The application process is immediate as soon as an internal or external candidate can complete whatever materials are required and push the *send* button. Because of technology, several companies have dramatically changed their application procedures. For example, for many companies, the process now involves an application video as opposed to, or in addition to, a letter of application and a résumé. I have no problem with this, and I feel there can be value to the video component of an online employment application. However, I also feel there is great continuing value in requiring a candidate to submit a résumé and a letter of application. As a matter of fact, my continuing recommendation is for this to be done as part of the application process, regardless of whatever else may be required. This provides the employer a look at the formal résumé and writing skills of the candidate. If a company is uncomfortable with the video application process for any of a variety of reasons, this can be stopped; however, I do understand that video is becoming a more popular part of the digital online application process.

The point is that whatever electronic process is used to facilitate the application, it is still my recommendation that an application form of some type be utilized and the candidate be required to submit a résumé with a letter of application. These materials can be electronically transferred or sent via conventional mail. These processes are important, because while we have amazing communication advantages today that are beyond anything previous generations dreamed, it is still very important for people to possess the ability to communicate effectively both orally and through writing.

There should also always be an application deadline in force, regardless of procedures. It should be made clear that applications received after that deadline will not be considered. If you want a job, there is no excuse for missing an application deadline. I also believe the company or association application form should provide a phone number and a contact person a candidate can call after the application deadline, to follow up on the status of his or her employment application. A good candidate will follow up with a phone call or at least an e-mail to ensure his or her application has been received and to ask if any further information is needed.

I mention a phone call because there is great value in the candidate actually speaking to someone (whether it be a potential supervisor or HR person) designated to take those calls. This can provide an employer further insight into the verbal abilities of the candidate, how the candidate handles him- or herself in that situation, and whether or not the candidate does follow up on tasks. I would offer this important note to candidates: it is necessary for you to conduct the follow-up contact in an efficient, professional manner, but you should not be a pest after that initial follow-up. The last thing any human resources employee or supervisor desires is a phone call from you every day for two weeks while he or she is trying to consider whom to hire. Yet, a well-done, professional telephone call from a candidate (after the application process has closed) is an excellent idea to check signals with the potential employer and see if anything else is needed. That call is an opportunity to ask the obvious question about when a possible decision might be made in regard to filling the position. There is a difference between a phone call like that and being a pest. It is amazing how many people do not understand the difference. Being impatient can, and usually does, cause a candidate problems.

Here is a note for employers regarding references. While candidates usually provide references, I have found that references are often useless. Let's state the obvious: any candidate is obviously going to make sure his or her references only include individuals who will give glowing recommendations. The other obvious reality is that some individuals serving as references are often very cautious about what they say to a potential employer. That is not to say the reference would be untruthful, but the reference is often very selective about what he or she says. There is a difference, one the potential employer needs to understand and take into consideration when calling references provided by candidates.

The best way to check references is by utilizing the information provided on the résumé or application. If the individual worked for three different companies in the last four years, this might be a red flag. As an employer, I would call those three companies and speak directly with their respective human resources staff or the supervisor of the candidate. I realize this sounds fundamental, but I know that some companies simply call the references listed on the application form. As a potential employer, research a little deeper on your own, using information provided by the candidate.

The employer should study the candidate's résumé and make reference calls of his or her choosing. It is important to note that employers should make more than one or two calls, based on the résumé. Make four or five calls—it doesn't take that long, and you may be surprised what you learn. It is still possible the person you are calling for reference information may be very selective regarding what he or she tells you, but at least you will be doing your own research into the employment background and work habits of the candidate. There is also a variety of reliable services available that will do this work for an employer. Communication, as always, is extremely important. It is critical to hiring the right person and beginning an excellent relationship with that employee.

I have discussed some required efforts of candidates, and I have also discussed the application process and related procedures. The employer also has a great deal of obligation in this process. It seems to me, after utilizing several different employment-application approaches and systems, that once applications are received from candidates, the employer has an obligation to respond immediately to the candidate(s), either in writing (electronically or otherwise) or with a telephone call. Again, I recommend the phone call to let the candidate know personally that his or her materials have been received. At that time, the candidate may ask follow-up questions, as recommended earlier in this chapter. However, candidates should understand this should not replace their own follow-up phone call to be made later to determine if any further information is needed and to show the initiative to follow up and communicate with the potential employer.

The employer has an obligation in the follow-up communication to provide candidates with an approximate decision timeline. What is the expected (not guaranteed) time for the position to be filled, and are there other materials needed? The candidate needs to know the general timetable for filling the position or for the next step in the interview process. Nothing is worse for a candidate than wondering about the status of the position he or she applied for and receiving no communication from the employer. Let's be reasonable—this is not fair to the candidates. Most companies do a good job with their communications in this regard; however, it is something employers need to be reminded about.

When the time comes for the selected candidates to be interviewed, the company or association has an obligation to communicate clearly to those candidates, providing the necessary information regarding the interview location, what the candidate is expected to bring, and other pertinent details.

The company or association should also formally communicate with candidates not selected for an interview as soon as possible. This is a professional courtesy. Once again, I will recommend this be done via a phone call. This makes some people uncomfortable, but it is the right thing to do. Nothing is worse than being a candidate and hearing from a third party that the position you applied for has been filled. While sometimes difficult, you never go wrong communicating with people in a professional manner. The employer representative should call candidates not selected for an interview or for further consideration and express the appreciation of the company for their application, whether these were internal or external applicants. This puts forward a personal touch of appreciation from the company at a difficult time for the candidate who was not selected. It also provides an opportunity for the candidate to ask questions.

I believe candidates not selected for the position should ask where they fell short in securing the position. It is the responsibility of the employer to be prepared for these questions with reasonable, honest answers. Sometimes employers avoid this because it is uncomfortable. It is far more difficult for everyone, employer and candidate not selected, if the conversation does not take place for

More Common Sense

quite some time—or worse, never. With regard to who should call candidates not selected, it is often the policy of companies that the call be made by someone other than the supervisor for the position in question. I don't have strong feelings about this either way. I do not feel it is a requirement that the supervisor for the position make the call, and in some instances, that may not be appropriate. This depends on the specific situation. There is nothing inappropriate about a human-resources professional (trained in this area) communicating with candidates not selected. Again, this should be done (in my opinion) by telephone if possible. The contact should be made as quickly as possible. After the follow-up phone call is completed to the candidates not selected, the company should also follow up, with a letter sent conventionally or electronically, to the candidates not selected, thanking them for their interest in the company and for the opportunity of the follow-up phone conversation.

If the company feels a candidate not selected could be an excellent future candidate, then that letter (and the previous phone call) should include encouragement to the candidate to apply for future positions. If the company does not feel this way, then I recommend that no such statement be made. In the follow-up phone conversation, the candidate may ask if he or she should apply for another position with the company in the future. If the company representative feels there is value in a positive response to this, then so be it, but if this is not the case, the candidate should be informed up front. This just saves everyone time and hard feelings down the road. Far too often, candidates not chosen are told to apply again because the employer representative feels this "softens the blow." This is a bad idea. Be honest; in the long run, it is better for everyone.

There are many different approaches to dealing with candidates. What I have outlined in this chapter are a few very fundamental thoughts regarding the overall process. As always, the reader may or may not agree with these concepts. It is important to communicate with people, be fair, and conduct an equitable application process. It remains very important to evaluate the oral and written skills of candidates. A résumé is still important, and references should be handled by potential employers, as outlined in this chapter. Surfacing candidates and meeting new people, whether they be internal or external candidates, should be an exciting and professionally conducted process for all parties involved.

Chapter 2

Interviewing Procedures

I remember my mentors' stories as they provided wisdom on interviewing procedures. There are a couple of stories I consider classic, and I am sure you have heard these. The first story is about the young man who came to an interview and did well in answering questions and interacting with the staff. However, he did not secure the position because there was mud on his trousers, and the condition of his shoes was deplorable. The young man obviously did not pay attention to detail. Is that a fair assessment of him or not?

The other classic story regards a young lady who had an interview that occurred at a luncheon, and the young lady salted her food before tasting it. She did not secure the position, because of the observation by the employment representative and, therefore, a lack of faith in the young lady's judgment. Is that a fair assessment of her or not?

You can make your own determinations about these stories and whether these individuals should have had their employment chances damaged by those actions. The process of interviewing, for the candidate and employer representative, often hinges a great deal on first impressions. This is not new. I always felt more weight should be placed on answers to questions and the substance of the interview discussion. However, upon reflection over the years, I agree both of the young people in the stories made errors. One error regarding the dress of the young man is obviously visible and should not have been made, as it had a negative effect on his first impression.

The second situation, involving the salting of the food, could be considered a lesser offense. However, it does convey a lack of judgment which, in that case, was concerning to the employer. In today's work environment, with casual dress and a variety of ever-changing rules pertaining to interviewing and employee behavior, some readers will consider these examples ridiculous or antiquated. I would submit that both of these examples have some merit and should indeed have at least some impact on the decision to interview those candidates further.

First impressions are extremely important. The first impression is usually made, especially in an employment interview, in the first twenty to thirty seconds when the employer representative and the candidate meet. We all need to understand this dynamic, and by the same token, a totally formed first impression probably occurs in the first fifteen to twenty minutes after dialogue has started between the parties.

Employment representatives need to be extremely observant of habits, body language, and other characteristics of a potential employee, along with the candidate's answers to interview questions. Candidates must understand that looks, habits, and other factors will have an impact on being selected for a position. Some readers may be saying, "We already knew this." That may be true, but it is always amazing how often candidates do not pay enough attention to these criteria.

The first and the final interview should always be conducted in private and one on one. This does not always happen. The interview itself is extremely important, along with information exchange and dialogue between the employer representative and the candidate. Often, associations or companies elect to conduct an interview in a public place, such as a restaurant: "Let's meet for lunch, and we can do the interview." I suppose conducting an interview at a restaurant is allowable, if and only if the individuals involved can secure a location that allows for privacy and productive, uninterrupted conversation. However, first and final interviews should really be conducted in an office or private location. Don't try to eat and interview. If, for whatever reason, there is not a comfort level with the interview being conducted at the office of the association or company, then make other arrangements to utilize a private office somewhere else. Secure a private office or venue at another business or conduct the interview at a library in a private conference room or any number of other locations. A private, uninterrupted interview is a professional service for both parties.

Formality should be part of the interview process, and conducting the first interview at a restaurant or public venue does not usually offer that opportunity. A second or a third interview, (if the process requires this), might be appropriate at a restaurant, but certainly not the first or last interview, when an offer of employment may be made.

I've heard association leaders and employers tell a candidate that he or she should bring his or her spouse along to the first interview. The theory of this approach is that the association leadership or employer representatives want to meet the spouse because he or she is part of the candidate's team, and they want to know the spouse supports the candidate. I understand, but quite honestly, I do not agree with this approach. It may be fine at a second or third interview or in a social setting. However, the spouse should definitely not be involved in the first interview. Association or corporate employers need to remember they are potentially hiring the candidate and not the spouse. I have seen this mistake made on many occasions and have witnessed the involvement of a spouse actually change the outcome of the first interview for the candidate—sometimes for the better and sometimes not.

Likewise, it is unadvisable after the first interview for the employer or the candidate to say, "Let's go out for a drink or a cup of coffee." Again, this is something that may be appropriate after an employment offer has been made and accepted. Both the candidate and the employer representative need to concentrate on first impressions and answers to questions. Being professionally friendly is important and necessary, but being friends—not only at the first interview but throughout the process of working together—can cause difficulties to some degree in an employee/supervisor relationship.

Remember that professional conduct is always required. The interview process is a two-way street. Often, employers feel the process is a one-way street, and it is "their way or the highway." Certainly, the employer has the upper hand, but there is also an obligation for the candidate to ask questions of the employer and for communication to flow freely back and forth between the employment representative and the candidate.

Employment representatives sometimes suggest to candidates that they meet for a meal prior to the interview itself. This doesn't work either. Once the two parties meet, from that moment forward, the interview is underway. The only time I would endorse a meal before an interview is when a third party is presenting multiple candidates for an interview with a potential employer, facilitating the interview process for the parties. In this case, it could be appropriate for the third party (not the representatives making the employment decisions) to meet with the candidates over a meal to discuss interview procedures.

In that case, if a meal is held in advance of the interview process, this could be appropriate and offer advantages toward helping the candidates relax and be prepared. However, if the employer representatives doing the hiring want to have a meal with the candidates prior to the interview, all this means is that the interview will be underway as soon as everyone arrives. It is also important to always interview candidates separately and privately. I have witnessed interviewing situations in which association or company employer reps wanted to interview candidates while other candidates were in the room. This is not fair to anyone, including the employer. Employers should always provide candidates the opportunity for a private interview.

Let's look at some preinterview subjects. Prior to the interview, candidates should receive information regarding the position.

How that information is sent to the candidate is irrelevant; just get them the information. Ideally, the candidate understands what the position is, or he or she would not have applied. Promising candidates will have done some homework on their own. However, prior to an interview, employers should provide candidates with an up-to-date copy of the job description, any code of ethics information for employees, and other materials pertinent to the company and the position. This should be done for both internal and external candidates. This is even more important, of course, to the external candidates who are not currently employed by the hiring organization or association. This information will help candidates prepare for the interview and allow the employer representative to ask specific questions to determine how well the candidate prepared for the interview, based on the materials the candidate received.

All background checks of candidates should be completed well before the first interview. Following the application process, the human-resources professionals at the association or company should have completed and filed reports on the employment checks, criminal checks, and other appropriate background information for each candidate.

The employer representative should never share information about individual candidates with other candidates. Again, this sounds like a fundamental no-brainer, but I have seen this violated on occasion. I have heard of employer representatives even discussing who else was applying for a position; of course, every candidate applying for a position wants to know who else has applied. Besides that, especially regarding internal candidates, it is most likely that the rumor mill or grapevine has already provided everyone in the company with that information. This is not easily controllable.

The point is, the employer representative conducting the interviews should never provide information about one candidate to another candidate. Also, the candidates should never inquire about other employees applying for the position. That, as far as I am concerned, is an unethical question from the candidate and a deal breaker.

Candidates should have all information regarding interview procedures and expectations provided to them ahead of time. However, one special area needs to be discussed. This is an area that often becomes confusing and could place one candidate at an advantage over another because of a lack of communication. Advance communication to candidates must clearly state whether candidates are allowed to bring samples of their work to an interview. In the case of a strictly management position, such as a program-director position, this could be samples of writing or program-development work. This would be self-explanatory in the case of a graphic artist, which would involve samples of artwork created, etc.

Whatever the situation, the employer representative does not want to find him- or herself in a situation in which he or she is interviewing candidates and considering some candidates based on work samples or portfolio information they brought, without having that same information from other candidates. Keep all candidates on an even playing field with the same rules when it comes to interviews.

Let's move into the next area of work that should be completed prior to the interview and communicated to each employee privately. This area can be controversial. If an employer truly wants to consider all candidates on a level playing field, this should include communicating the basic compensation package to each candidate prior to the interview process. In other words, the compensation and benefit package for a position should be established for that position, as determined by sound, market-based analysis conducted by the human-resources and management professionals for the company. This should not be negotiated before the first interview with any candidates. This approach is not always favored by many in management, but this is especially important before the first interview. During the hiring process, there may be a point, especially after a second or third interview, when an employer needs or desires to discuss fine-tuning the compensation package. When the interview process gets to this point, such discussion may be entirely appropriate. It may be desirable and necessary to discuss any flexible components of the compensation package, such as compensation, should this be necessary to hire the desired candidate. Some components of a compensation package can be flexible. For example, if necessary during the final interview, there may be some flexibility regarding salary or moving expenses. This is fine as long as those negotiations are within the employment procedures and guidelines of the company or association.

Let's again take salary as an example. If a job is posted at a certain salary, that salary should be communicated to all candidates, along with other compensation package information prior to the first interview. Every candidate should understand that information. The job in question may have a salary range; most likely, this is the case. Should negotiation become necessary in the second or third interview to procure a desired candidate, some salary negotiation could be appropriate, depending on the specific situation. However, that negotiation should always stay within the established salary range for that position—because this is fair to the other candidates and fair to existing employees.

The company should not violate its established vacation policy or provide the desired candidate with a more attractive policy than currently exists for the company or association. This type of activity would be unfair to current employees. Vacation policy is one of those subjects that is inflexible. Some people may disagree. Salary negotiation in the eleventh hour of interviewing discussions may be somewhat flexible, as long as that flexibility follows human-resources guidelines and, again, is within the company-determined salary range for the position.

It is never appropriate to negotiate with candidates prior to or during the first interview, and usually not even during the second interview. When the employer does this, they open themselves up to a very difficult situation. When this negotiation is allowed so early in the interview process, the employer may lose focus of what its first task should be. The employer should be concentrating on finding the best person to fill the position. This includes talent, background, education, experience, communication skills, and a variety of other considerations. That process should not be tainted by the fact that one employee has submitted his or her application with a salary expectation of $45,000 and the other has submitted his or her application with a salary expectation of $52,000. When this type of information is allowed at the very beginning of the interview process, it probably will skew the candidate-evaluation process on the part of the employer. In other words, the employer may hire a candidate who is less qualified for the position because he or she is willing to accept less compensation. If the interview process is correctly conducted to surface the best candidate, then at the beginning of the interview process, this should not be a factor. Having said that, as I stated before, all candidates for a position should be aware of what the *posted* salary is for that position and what the overall components of the compensation package are. Some people will disagree, but my commentary is based on many years of hiring and interviewing experience from a practical standpoint. If employers do decide to ask candidates to submit a salary expectation, that number should be within the salary range for the position.

Candidates should be interviewed by utilizing similar, or preferably *the same* questions. This is not an exact science because the background or experiences of an individual are, of course, very important to interview questions, and discussions will vary somewhat from candidate to candidate. However, it is extremely important, especially in the first interview, for all candidates to be asked similar questions and to be provided with basically the same amount of time for the initial interview. This provides the employer representative or an association or corporate board with a fair first impression of each candidate. Again, the level playing field for all candidates is important.

It is now time to move into commentary regarding the interview itself. We have already covered the fact that each candidate should receive information on the position, including information about the company or association, the job description, and the compensation package. That packet should also include information regarding the logistics of the interview procedure.

It is very important that both the candidate and the employer representative prepare prior to the interview process. This should go without saying, but often because of time constraints or other considerations, this does not occur. Both parties should consider their attire and how they will look for the interview. Both the employer representative and the candidate should consider what questions need to be asked and have those questions prepared prior to the interview. It is important for both parties to consider what questions are appropriate and pertinent to the interview process. I once experienced a situation in which an employer representative asked a candidate if she had a boyfriend, to which the candidate replied, "No." The employer representative then proceeded to ask the young lady, "If you did have a boyfriend, how do you *think* he would feel about the time constraints associated with the travel for this position?" That is a terrible and inappropriate question. It is important for the employer representative and the candidate to prepare correct, ethical questions that pertain to the position.

Both parties should be prepared to take notes if needed; however, excessive note-taking during the interview process can be very distracting. It is better for both parties to make very brief notes during the process. If the parties feel compelled to make detailed notes, this should be done immediately following the interview. The employer representative should be prepared to answer questions regarding the job description and the expectations for the position. The candidate should be prepared to answer questions regarding his or her résumé and qualifications, as well as willingness to travel or relocate, and so on.

I have conducted effective first interviews in thirty to forty-five minutes. Still, it is my opinion this can be too short a period, but it depends on the position and the candidate. Certainly, a first interview should never go beyond one hour; the forty-five-minute timeframe is usually the appropriate length of time for the first interview. It is quite conceivable and perhaps appropriate for a second or third interview to go longer, but not the first interview.

There are many effective ways to conduct the actual interview. I like to follow an approach that has worked well for me.

Here are some basic procedures for a *first* interview:

- The employer representative should ask the candidate to introduce him- or herself and provide opening remarks after the employer representative has welcomed the candidate and made him or her feel comfortable. Water should always be available for everyone.
- The candidate should provide opening remarks he or she feels are appropriate. This will tell the employer representatives a great deal about the candidate from several vantage points. The candidate should be able to provide opening comments in a couple of minutes. A candidate

who makes opening comments for fifteen minutes can hurt him- or herself in the interview process.

- Following the opening comments by the candidate, the employer representative should begin asking the candidate questions for approximately twenty-five to thirty minutes. Time is needed during this portion of the interview process for interaction. On a limited basis, there can be time for the candidate not only to answer the questions specifically but also offer brief commentary relevant to the question.
- Following the question-and-answer period led by the employer representative, the candidate should be provided an opportunity to ask the employer representative questions he or she feels are important. This will provide the employer representative with insight into the candidate's preparation for the interview. I would recommend the candidate not ask ten questions but rather be prepared to ask three or four excellent questions.
- At this point in the first interview, the employer representative should thank the candidate for his or her interest in the position and review the timetable for the decision-making process. The candidate should know when he or she may hear something back from the employer representative regarding further consideration.

Should questions come up regarding the compensation package, those certainly should be answered, but given the fact that the candidate should already know the basic established compensation package, the first interview is not a place for detailed discussion about the compensation package by either the employer representative or the candidate. There will be time for that in the future. Again, the candidate should know the compensation package and be interested enough in the position (from that vantage point) to have applied. The employer representative should show the candidate out of the office area or the building. Both parties should always extend professional courtesy.

Conducting the interview process correctly in a formal setting provides the same opportunity to all candidates. This also allows the employer representative to evaluate candidates equitably.

The final commentary in this chapter deals with communication and follow-up. For anyone familiar with my work, this will be no surprise. This addresses the professional nature of both the employer representative and the candidate. Communication following the first interview is very important. The candidate has a need to know within the shared timeframe whether or not he or she will be considered further for the position. Remember, nothing is worse for a candidate than to wonder what is going on and receive no communication from the employer. It is best to do this by phone, as noted earlier. This does not need to be a long conversation if the candidate is not being considered further.

The employer representative making the call should be prepared to answer questions about why the candidate is not going to be considered further. Following that telephone call, it is important to follow up with written communication. In the case of the candidate who will not be considered further, the written communication should consist of a thank-you showing appreciation for the candidate's interest in the position. If the employer deems it appropriate, a statement encouraging the candidate to apply for positions in the future could be included. If the employer does not feel this way, the employer should absolutely not place that in the communication or state this verbally or on the phone.

This follow-up communication is very important and brings closure to the situation for the candidate not chosen. It also provides confirmation of logistical information for the candidate moving forward in the interview process.

I always felt conducting interviews was as privilege and was quite interesting. It was an opportunity to meet people and learn more about existing employees. It was often an opportunity to discover new ideas and bring a new individual to the employment team. That is exciting. It is important that the process be conducted fairly and professionally from beginning to conclusion.

Chapter 3

Starting the New Job

You applied for the position, and you have been hired. You did your research on the position and prepared for the interview. You were successful. Great! Before you arrive for the first day of your new position, you need to do more research. Make sure you are aware of the organizational staffing structure, including supervisor levels pertaining to your position. Gather information about the expectations of the position and the challenges that exist. This can be gained through conversations with your new supervisor before your first day on the job. The human-resources professionals can also assist. There is so much information available today, and the speed of communication is so incredibly immediate that gathering this data is not difficult—but it is still something you need to facilitate.

After you prepare yourself with this further information, you should make a list of questions you would like to have answered upon starting your new position. You will most likely not get answers to all of your questions on the first day. However, showing your supervisor that you have been giving this thought and letting him or her know you have a list of questions you would like to have answered shows excellent preparation and organizational skills. It sends a clear message that you want to do the very best job you can.

However, there is a procedural caution regarding your question list. Before you start down your list of questions, it is wise to see how many of those questions are already answered in materials you have received. Most supervisors do not like answering the same question twice. Following orientation, you may find you have several questions that still need to be answered. If your company has a good employee orientation program, then I suspect many of your questions will be answered at that time. Unfortunately, it has been my experience that internal company candidates moving from one position to another, often do not receive enough orientation about a new position. However, this is needed. This responsibility usually falls on the human-resources professionals facilitating the hiring process and/or your new supervisor.

On the first day (and all subsequent days), it is important to be on time. I am amazed how many people have difficulty with this fundamental requirement. As I have mentioned in other

More Common Sense

comments, being on time means being five minutes early, not twenty-five minutes early and certainly not late. Of course, attire is very important. Part of your research should be to understand the company rules on dress. Your attire on the first day (and every day) should be correct. It would be my recommendation that if anything, your attire should be slightly better than required, but you don't need to overdo it.

You should always be prepared to take notes. Taking notes can make some people nervous, but it is a great way to remember and later study the information from a meeting, including assignments you have been asked to complete. I always took notes, and I received a great deal of pleasure from going down my list each day and crossing everything off that I had accomplished. Most people in management have this trait; it is something comes naturally for organized people. I always redrafted and updated my to-do list each day.

Be courteous to everyone. You must also appear confident that you are able to accomplish your new duties, but you must not appear arrogant. Never comment about others who applied for the job, even though you should not know who those people are. If you are in a normal association or corporate environment, you probably knew every one of the internal job candidates soon after the job posting went up. Unfortunately, this is the way of the world. Always take the high road with your attitude and try to work effectively with others.

Plan to do a tremendous amount of listening. If you have been placed in a promotion position and you now have several employees reporting to you, it is very important that you schedule individual, private discussion time with each person as appropriate within the reporting structure for both the salaried and hourly-wage employees under your supervision. People like to be listened to. Don't get me wrong—they also want to hear your thoughts, but you should know as a supervisor that they really want you to listen to their ideas, compliments, and concerns.

As you move into your new position, if you have employees reporting to you, never make promises you can't keep. A common mistake of new (and some experienced) supervisors is to begin making promises specifically to gain popularity with employees. When those promises cannot be fulfilled, trouble presents itself. Listen to what people have to say, and engage in conversation with them. I have been in many private meetings with employees who made requests. At the end of the meeting, the request was not granted, and still the employee considered the meeting a success because I listened to his or her request and why it was important to the employee.

When it was impossible to fulfill the request, I didn't just say no. Instead I explained, within the parameters of my position, why the request was not approved. Plan to do a lot of listening throughout your career. Many very successful people know the following quotation: "You learn nothing new when you are talking." This can be really challenging for someone who enjoys his or her position with great passion and is busting at the seams to offer suggestions or surface new ideas. Never underestimate the value of having passion and true enthusiasm for what you do. If it is genuine, it will show immediately and can be your greatest asset.

As a new employee, adopt an immediate "I will not talk about others" philosophy. Whether or not you are new to a position, participating in company gossip will eventually become a performance issue. Beyond that, especially while you are learning the lay of the land, it is highly advisable not to talk about someone else negatively. A great deal of good judgment is needed here, depending upon your level of experience, who you are with, and what the conversation entails. Ethics overrules everything, and the old phrase "praise in public and criticize in private" has a lot of merit. Also, you need to exercise caution in this area, especially in your capacity as an employee or a staff member to a new position. It is important to remember you have no idea who is friends with someone else or who is related or what the professional work dynamics are between the employees throughout your department or division. Give yourself a break. Learn the lay of the land before you even consider talking about someone, and actually, don't do it anyway—it's just not a good idea.

As a new employee, it is also beneficial, especially in your first days, not to offer multiple new suggestions to those above you in the chain of command, unless you are asked or something critical arises that needs your attention. You should feel free and be encouraged to offer suggestions in the future, but learn the job first. There are always exceptions to these communication rules based on good judgment, which you must possess in order to be promoted and successful. As a matter of fact, good judgment is probably one of the factors that led to you receiving the job. It is extremely important to understand the internal company or association dynamics of your position and of those you report to before you begin offering suggestions. Allow yourself the important advantage of understanding the job and the company structure before you proceed.

You should also be prepared in your first days to tell people a little about yourself. Other employees are usually curious about the new person, and you should be prepared to provide a brief synopsis of your background. Unfortunately, I have seen people answer this question using anywhere from thirty to forty-five minutes. Unless they have been specifically asked to do so, people generally stop listening, especially today, after about one or two minutes. One of the dynamics that is very evident today and very challenging is people's lack of attention span. This has developed gradually through advances in a wide variety of electronic communication technology, including social media. People used to enjoy listening to someone talk for an hour, and that is (with exceptions pertaining to truly outstanding speakers), just not the case in business operations anymore. Yet, this remains somewhat challenging at times because it often takes more than a two-minute conversation to explain a situation or assignment or even provide background information about yourself. When giving information about yourself, try to keep it to a minute, perhaps less. Then provide people an opportunity to ask questions, which allows your audience to control their time.

Make sure you are respectful to everyone you meet. You may have heard something about someone and therefore have a preconceived notion about that person. Remember that the preconceived notion came to you as an opinion of someone else. You may file that opinion in the back of your mind, but you need to judge for yourself. You may find you don't agree with that opinion, or the opposite could be true. People also have every right to a different opinion than you have. The fact that someone has a different opinion than you does not make him or her a bad person; the differing opinion may not be wrong. This person simply has a different opinion, and that is all. Obviously, you are not required to follow others' advice or to take action based on their opinion. The exception to this, of course, is when your supervisor gives you direction under normal circumstances.

Finally, on a logistical point, take time to learn the layout of the building or the physical plan for the facility, if you are not already familiar. For your own safety and daily use, try to arrange for a building tour to become familiar with the floor plan, including emergency exits, restrooms, and offices you will need to frequent. This may sound like a fundamental idea, but it does not always happen without your request.

Keep a calendar of dates and deadlines, and adhere to it. Keep it in your smartphone or, as is the case with many people I know, carry a conventional calendar. It doesn't matter how you do it—just do it. Especially as a new employee, your calendar should not only include meetings and face-to-face obligations but should also include deadlines for assignments and other information. You need to familiarize yourself with the company intranet if the company has one, and most do today. If you were previously employed with the company, you are already probably familiar with this, but if your role in the company has changed or you came from the outside, it will be important for you to become familiar with the company intranet immediately, so you can keep up with announcements and information.

These may be common-sense remarks and suggestions, but it is amazing how often they are not followed, causing difficulty that could otherwise have been easily avoided. Start your new position off by just using a lot of good common sense.

Chapter 4

The Purposes and Mechanics of Performance Reviews

The performance-review process is often misunderstood and even feared, not only by the employee but also by the supervisor. Generally speaking, most people don't like to do performance reviews, and this includes both supervisors and employees. The opposite should be true. The performance review is, first and foremost, a communication process and a great opportunity for uninterrupted communication between an employee and his or her supervisor. It is time set apart from regular, hectic, day-to-day duties, when the supervisor and the employee can and should engage in uninterrupted quality conversation regarding the duties of the employee. The process should also include discussion on the employee/supervisor professional working relationship. This should be a respectful, professional, and confidential conversation. It is a discussion both parties should look forward to conducting.

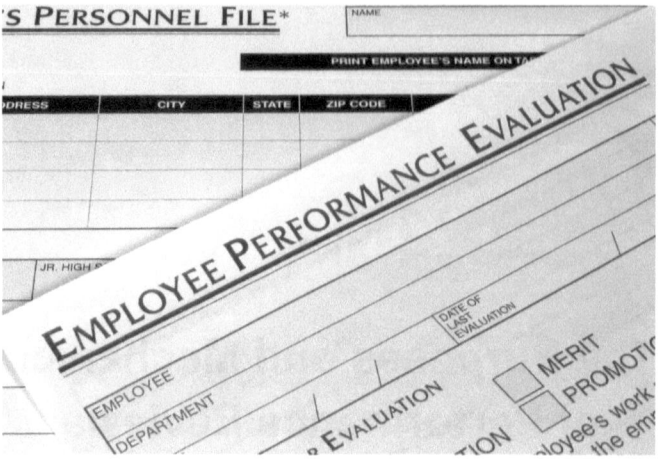

There are several segments to correctly conducting a performance review process and discussion. The supervisor and employee should hold the performance review discussion in an environment that is private and free from interruption. Some performance reviews are done over an extended lunch at a restaurant or other location. I have no problem with this, as long as the setting allows for confidential discussion that is not hurried. However, it can be challenging to eat and discuss. If you do this eat first and then discuss.

In preparation for a performance review, both parties are required to do some homework. There should be a professional performance-review form, which both the supervisor and the employee should review prior to meeting. This form should set forward discussion topics with an order and procedures for the performance review. In other words, both parties should prepare for the review by being familiar with the questions and discussion points that make up the performance-review process. The performance review should also include a review of the job description for the employee, to make sure it is still correct. The review process should include an evaluation of the employee's accomplishments, based on the previously established objectives for the past year. It should include discussion and determination of objectives for the coming year. The discussion can also include the employee's possible future employment desires. I refer to these points as my seven points of success for a performance review. To summarize:

1. Utilize an approved professional performance-review form and procedure to facilitate the process. Both the employee and supervisor should prepare ahead by reviewing the discussion topics and process.
2. Review the job description of the employee. Be prepared to make changes as needed.
3. Review and evaluate the employee objectives and accomplishments for the past year.
4. Review and determine the employee objectives for the coming year.
5. Hold a respectful discussion between supervisor and employee regarding the day-to-day realities of the employee and supervisor professional working relationship.
6. Discussion should include an opportunity for the employee to talk about future employment desires.
7. Performance reviews should not be hurried and should be confidential.

There is also an eighth optional point that can be reviewed if it exists: the update and review of an individual development plan for the employee, if (and only if) the employee has embraced that concept. In the next chapter, I discuss employee individual development plans in detail.

The performance-review form itself can take many different approaches. There are many types of forms and procedures that can be used. It is important to choose one, to establish order for your meeting. The discussion may also include decisions about future training that could benefit the employee. These training needs may be included in the future objectives for the employee. The performance-review form should include a discussion to surface concerns and compliments about how the employee interacts with other employee team members and leaders. There should be an opportunity for discussion specifically regarding employee attitude, which without a doubt, can be one of the most difficult subjects for employees and supervisors to discuss.

The completed performance-review form should be signed by both the employee and the supervisor. The supervisor has the responsibility to write up the performance review for the employee, using the form chosen. The final write-up for the performance review should be reviewed by the supervisor and the employee together, prior to both parties signing. In addition to the completed performance-review form, the process should include several supplemental documents. It *must* include a review of the job description by both parties, noting updates or changes. The evaluation of past objectives and the new employee objectives can be included as separate attached documents or included on the performance-review form if the form allows space for that.

The discussion regarding the employee's future employment desires is of special importance to the employee. Supervisors need to understand that facilitating this discussion as a part of the performance-review process sends a great message to the employee that you and the association or company are paying attention to that employee and considering him or her for promotion. Nothing is more important to most employees than an understanding that supervisors genuinely care about their professional growth and development. Regarding the discussion on the future of the employee, it is important to document this information on the performance-review form. Most performance-review forms have a place for general commentary. There should also be a place on the form for the employee to provide comments. Allowing the employee to do so also sends a very positive message to the employee. It says the association does care about his or her opinions. Far too often, companies or associations do not make this part of the performance-review form and discussion.

As stated, there are many different styles of performance-review forms available. Many companies have developed their own form and process through their human resources departments, while other companies or associations have purchased performance-review packages from professional firms. As long as the form is legally correct and is provided to both parties before the discussion and facilitates professional discussion opportunities in the aforementioned subject areas, I think almost any form could be used.

When it comes to reviewing employee objectives for the past year and determining objectives for the coming year, it is important to remember that objectives must have certain characteristics to be of value. Objectives must be clear and understood by both the supervisor and the employee. There must be complete understanding regarding what each objective is and what will be deemed as successful achievement of the objectives. It is very important that objectives be *measurable* if possible. Sometimes this can be difficult, especially regarding more subjective objectives. Often in membership associations or association-management situations, as opposed to traditional corporate situations, this can be challenging. However, there are ways for both parties to understand what measurable actions must take place in order for objectives to be considered achieved. If the objective can be measured, this provides greater clarity for both parties and will limit the opportunity for misunderstanding when it comes time to determine if the objective was attained.

Objectives should also be listed in priority order. Prioritizing objectives provides the employee an opportunity to understand what is most important to his or her supervisor and to the company or association. As objectives are discussed during the employee performance review, the prioritization helps facilitate the discussion in a more productive and organized manner. Objectives should not be lengthy and should be stated in a sentence or two if possible. Objectives should contain action verbs, which clearly indicate to the employee what action or activities need to be taken and what accomplishments are expected to achieve success. I recommend that no employee have more than seven to ten annual prioritized major objectives. This does not mean that employees would only have seven to ten things to do for the year—not at all. All of the employee duties should be covered in the job description, which, by the way, should be prioritized as well. However, when establishing employee major objectives, it is important to limit the list to the top seven to ten most important achievements that the supervisor expects the employee to accomplish in the coming year. This provides greater direction to the employee.

During the review process, the most important discussion can be the review of the employee performance objectives for the past year and establishing objectives for the coming year. The discussion of those two issues is the heart of the performance review. This is not to understate the importance of the review of the job description, which is fundamental to the entire process, or the discussion regarding future employment opportunities. However, as we look at the pure reason for the performance-review process, it is to assess the effectiveness and productivity of the employee for the past year and to set forth objectives based on the job description and company priorities for the coming year. Any performance-review process that does not include an evaluation of past objectives and the establishment of future objectives would be flawed, to say the least.

The discussion regarding future employment opportunities or desires can and should be a much more subjective discussion. This is an important opportunity for the employee to provide commentary to his or her supervisor about positions of interest for the future or to ask questions about future employment opportunities. This may include transfers within the company and other related subjects. Employees are often reluctant to engage in the future-discussion commentary because they fear stepping on someone's toes or coming across in an undesirable manner. This is where the supervisor must show flexibility and an aptitude for facilitating the performance-review discussion. The supervisor must make the employee feel comfortable with the discussion process and these topics. Trust becomes a huge factor (as it always is) in this discussion between supervisor and employee. To the extent that trust is achieved, this will have a great bearing on the discussion regarding future employment changes or opportunities. If there is solid, noteworthy information that comes out of this discussion, it should be documented in the results of the performance review. There is value in doing this because it shows the employee that the supervisor has heard what he or she has stated and has documented the employee's comments.

The next chapter deals with individual development plans (IDPs). While an individual development plan is not necessarily part of the regular performance review form or process, it can be important to the performance discussion regarding future employment desires of the employee if an IDP is in place for that employee. The employee who is serious about future employment changes, including promotion or lateral movements, needs to understand that the completion of an individual development plan can be of extreme value to the employee, the supervisor, and the association or company. The supervisor has an obligation to make the employee aware of the IDP process if this exists. This individual development plan process involves real work and a commitment on behalf of the employee to work with the supervisor on his or her possible road map for the future. The supervisor needs to be proficient and clear in explaining the individual development plan process. Many companies do not offer an IDP process, and I think this is a mistake. The IDP can be a valuable career-planning tool for the employee and the association.

The individual development plan process provides an opportunity for an employee to develop a customized course of action specifically designed to pursue career development for that employee. It puts this plan on paper and creates an opportunity for the employee and supervisor to discuss this on a regular basis. While an IDP program (which can be developed by your HR professionals or purchased) provides the opportunity for a supervisor and employee to discuss future employment plans, there also needs to be an understanding by the employee that the individual development plan (and completion of the steps in the plan) does not guarantee a promotion or job change. This should not discourage employees. There are no guarantees, because company structures often change, budgets change, and other criteria can change, which can affect company objectives, staffing, and priorities. However, the employee needs to embrace the fact that the completion of an individual development plan does demonstrate initiative on his or her part to grow and continue being a part of the association.

It is important that the employee understands his or her individual development plan should contain several optional future employment avenues rather than establishing one rigid course of action. As I will discuss in the next chapter on IDPs, the employee who does not cultivate several options for growth and promotion will most likely become discouraged. The employee needs to understand the individual development plan's success rests on his or her shoulders. The employee must be fully engaged in the IDP process. While an individual development plan can and should be at least a part of the performance-review process, especially during the discussion regarding employee future employment desires, the IDP must also be reviewed and updated by the supervisor and employee in private discussion at least quarterly. Both the employee and the supervisor should feel good about making changes and updates to the plan. The IDP must be a living document that can be changed as needed whenever determined by the supervisor and employee.

I refer to the individual development plan in this chapter only in the context of how it can be important to the regular employee performance-review discussion regarding future employment desires of the employee. It is true that the individual development plan is and should be a separate document. I hope this chapter has shed some light on the very fundamental purposes and basic mechanics of performance reviews, a discussion that should be embraced by both the employee and the supervisor.

Chapter 5

The Individual Development Plan: Your Road Map

In the previous chapter, I discussed the individual development plan (IDP) and how that plan may fit into an employee performance review discussion. This chapter expands upon the subject. It is important to remember that an individual development plan is an optional career road map and professional development tool for an employee. The key to the success of an individual development plan is the buy-in and total commitment of the employee to the process and the support of the employee's supervisor. The supervisor and the employee must be willing to invest time and effort in the professional growth and development of the employee utilizing the individual development plan process.

There are several different types of individual development plan forms and procedures. What must an IDP include? The successful IDP must be a flexible document, in a manner of speaking, a living, breathing document that is totally embraced by the employee with the permission and support of the supervisor. The IDP must contain the following segments to be effective:

- ❖ Career-goal options (at least two or three preferable).
- ❖ Required steps to pursue each career-goal option.
- ❖ Action plans to pursue and achieve each of the required steps established.
- ❖ Formal evaluation and update of the IDP by the employee and supervisor on a quarterly basis.

It is imperative to understand (and many employees struggle with this and do not utilize an IDP for this reason) that having a working IDP does not guarantee a promotion. In the case of an IDP, some employees feel they should automatically receive a promotion when they successfully complete an individual development plan. This includes successful completion of the required steps for the various career-goal options via the action steps to facilitate success in those areas.

The employee who has an individual development plan demonstrates a seriousness about a long-term career with the company or association and a willingness to do extra work to prepare for promotion or lateral employment opportunities for which the employee demonstrates an aptitude and interest. The IDP demonstrates the work ethic of the employee and shows the employee is willing and capable of considering several options for promotion or lateral movement. When a promotion or a lateral opportunity of interest to the employee comes available, supervisors should absolutely take into consideration the employee who has been successfully committed to the IDP process.

It is imperative for both employee and supervisor to understand that the individual development plan must remain flexible. The plan itself and the actions of the employee, supported by the supervisor, are always subject to corporate or association staffing or structural changes and economic changes. It is conceivable that an employee and his or her supervisor may want to meet monthly to review the employee IDP, especially if the employee is engaged in one or more action plans to pursue the required steps for the various career-goal options listed in the IDP. The discussion regarding an IDP and the utilization of such a plan should be a confidential matter between the employee and supervisor. It is important that supervisors understand the IDP process should be made available to all employees having a genuine interest in promotion opportunities or lateral opportunities. This should include employment opportunities that may exist with a subsidiary or affiliated company. Regardless of what process or form is used for an individual development plan (many companies create their own form and procedure), it is important that the IDP include the steps outlined in this chapter. Let's review each of these steps in further detail.

When we consider career-goal options, the employee must understand that because of the ever-changing corporate or association environment and the world around us, there is a real advantage to having a career road map in place that contains perhaps two or three possible different routes to growth and success. Too many employees focus on one future job or position. They are fixed on just one job, and when something happens that eliminates that possibility, they become upset, sometimes to the point of discontinuing their career with the company or becoming bitter with a poor attitude. This, of course, gains the employee and the company nothing. It also raises another interesting point about individual development plans.

An IDP itself does not necessarily measure all the important factors that must be considered in any employee promotion or lateral change. These is also employee enthusiasm, dedication, commitment, and loyalty. The employee who excels in these areas will be successful and can make up for some skill set deficiencies. Not only do employees need to strive to achieve these characteristics, but supervisors need to aggressively promote the importance of these employee characteristics. While these characteristics always play into an IDP (because those are the types of employees who generally want to do an IDP), the plan itself, with its career options, required steps, and action plans, does not necessarily always adequately measure the qualities of dedication, loyalty, and commitment of the employee. The IDP process itself may not do a good enough job of measuring specific leadership characteristics. For example, the employee who achieves all of the required steps via action plans for career options as outlined in his or her IDP but has a poor attitude should not be a candidate for a promotion or even a lateral change, depending on the specific situation.

More Common Sense

The career-goal options of the employee can be whatever the employee and the supervisor agree to, within the parameters of reality. Obviously, in some membership associations, employees are not eligible for elected leadership positions but are eligible for other staff positions. Factors such as this need to be taken into consideration. When it comes to career-goal options, the employee and the supervisor need to be realistic. These options need to be promotion or lateral options that genuinely excite the employee (at least at the time of inclusion in the IDP) and are realistic.

Some of you may ask why I keep including lateral employment possibilities. You may feel there is no excitement unless a promotion is the goal. While many people do feel that way, other employees may have lateral employment goals based on a certain job they feel they could have a passion for. It is important to remember that employee goals in an individual development plan do not have to be promotion based but might be lateral based as well. This depends on employee aspirations and the ongoing discussion between the employee and his or her supervisor.

Regarding the action plans needed to achieve required steps, this is where the rubber meets the road. These action steps are the most important part of the IDP process. For each required step to achieve a career goal, there should be a listing of the *measurable actions* needed to achieve that step. This is the IDP phase where the real work exists. It is during this phase that the employee may need to complete a training course or travel assignment or a special project. These are the action plan steps that must be clear and understood by the employee and the supervisor. The measurability of these action steps is vitally important so the employee and supervisor can understand and accurately determine if progress is being made.

The last area an IDP must include is the ongoing evaluation phase of the overall plan itself. Some employees and supervisors meet monthly to discuss the IDP, but that can be a significant commitment. It also may not be necessary, as the conversation could become redundant on a monthly basis if nothing much has changed from the previous meeting. Having said that, I will stress that meeting at least quarterly is important. Once a year is not enough. The status of an existing IDP should be discussed as a part of the employee's annual performance review in the "future plans" section. When the IDP is reviewed on a quarterly basis by the employee and supervisor, it is important for both parties to make adjustments to keep the IDP on track.

As you can see, an individual development plan must be a living document. It must be flexible and allow for change. It can be a valuable career-planning and development tool that demonstrates the interest of the employee in employment change, including promotion. It does, in my opinion, give that employee an advantage when a promotion comes available. Some excellent employees don't want to do an individual development plan. They cite a business world that changes too often for any kind of an employee development plan to be of value. I disagree. I have always felt strongly that advance planning, whether it be career planning, program planning, or financial planning, has value and is necessary, even when we know changes affecting these plans will undoubtedly occur. Adjustments can always be made. We all know things can and will change, but that doesn't mean we should sit around and plan nothing in regard to preparation and organizing our thoughts about how we may proceed depending upon what happens. Your career planning and professional development are too important.

Chapter 6

Employee Performance Problems and Terminations

To say that employee terminations can be difficult would be an understatement. On occasion, dealing with terminations is a duty a supervisor is expected to carry out in a professional manner.

If performance reviews for the employee, including discussions about performance problems, have been documented and communicated correctly, it should be evident to an employee that continuing performance problems could eventually lead to termination. Still, termination sometimes seems to come as a surprise to some employees. Some employees who were furious at the time of termination return later and indicate their departure from the company was probably the best thing that could have happened because they were not a good fit for the job and were not happy. While this is not usually the case, it does happen.

More Common Sense

Employees having performance problems should immediately have discussions with their supervisors upon the negative performance issues being raised. Waiting or procrastination just makes things worse. Performance problems must be part of the annual employee performance review discussion, but supervisors and employees should understand they do not need to wait until the annual performance review to have a discussion about employee performance.

Another challenging aspect that supervisors need to guard against is the possible impact of other employees in the performance review discussion between a supervisor and a specific employee. Supervisors need to disregard the opinions of other employees who have no relevance to the performance review for another employee. Sometimes those opinions may not be motivated by fact but rather by personality differences or other factors. Performance issues needing improvement should be discussed in a private session between the employee and supervisor. In addition, it is important that both the employee and the supervisor hold each other's confidence as they move forward to address and correct performance issues. The first course of action for both supervisor and employee is to communicate and attempt to correct the problems. There should always be significant effort put forth to this end unless the performance issues are of a specific, very severe nature.

Certain procedures should be followed in any discussion regarding performance challenges. Many different forms and procedures are available. It is important that employee performance problems be documented and clearly understood by both the supervisor and the employee. It is important that the employee receive documentation of the performance review problems from the supervisor. Both the employee and the supervisor should retain signed copies. The documentation and related information should include specific actions to be taken to correct the performance issues. This information should also include a specific date when the supervisor and employee will meet again to review progress being made in the challenging performance review areas.

Sometimes, when reviewing performance problems, the above procedures do not happen because one or both parties don't follow through. Supervisors may not want to document information, and if it later becomes necessary to terminate an employee, there can be cloudy areas and confusion. This can delay the entire process because proper documentation and clarity of performance issues needing improvement were not professionally communicated, as the employee in question may attest in defense of his or her position. Supervisors need to make sure this does not happen. Necessary actions for corrective performance measures must be clear and, if possible, measurable, so both parties involved can determine and understand progress.

If performance discussions and documentations occur off cycle of the annual employee performance review, it is important that these papers be part of the employee personnel file and part of the next regular annual performance-review discussion.

I cannot overemphasize the need for any termination action to be preceded by clear documentation of problems and fair, accurate communications with the employee. This is fair to the employee and is the correct approach. Properly terminating an employee—and before that action, properly communicating with the employee regarding performance problems that needed to be corrected—reduces risk for the company and is also fair to the employee.

Regarding documentation of performance problems and courses of action for the employee to make corrections, I prescribe to the "three strikes and you're out" process. I do this not because I'm a former baseball player or because it's a catchy phrase, but because this approach provides a good, fair, step-by-step communication process with the employee. The company or association should always demonstrate a fair and reasonable approach toward the employee.

Please note that regarding the three strikes procedures, I am referring to employees with performance-review problems that are not, obviously, of a fraud or mismanagement nature. Employees having committed acts of harassment, financial mismanagement, or other serious actions can and should be dismissed immediately if the specific situation clearly warrants that action. In other words, there are situations where the dismissal of an employee should be immediate. Those situations are usually obvious, and any supervisor will no doubt receive assistance from his or her human-resources professionals and others. I restate now that this chapter is about normal performance problems having to do with failures dealing with job duties, assignments, employee attitude, etc.

Let's return to the three strikes and you're out approach. Fundamentally, what does this mean? Strike one—this is when the supervisor and employee first officially discuss the employee performance problems. Documentation occurs, the employee and supervisor agree on a course of action to correct the problems, and they agree on a time to meet again. Hopefully, when they meet again, the problems are solved, and everyone moves on.

However, if the performance problems still exist when they meet again, the next step, the second strike, comes into play. This time, documentation from the supervisor indicates that the employee, upon not fulfilling his or her duties appropriately, may have a future discussion with the supervisor regarding termination. It is in this second phase that the employee now officially understands what action *may* be taken if he or she does not successfully correct the performance problems. The documentation in this phase again includes the signatures of both the employee and the supervisor and the specific time designated to meet again to review progress.

Let's say the employee performance problems continue when the employee returns for the third meeting. If employee performance has not improved (and especially if performance has further deteriorated), this can be the third strike. It is during this step that the supervisor may or may not elect, based upon his or her judgment, to terminate the employee. If termination happens, it should be done face to face in a brief, straightforward manner. Once again, company human-resources professionals can help in this regard. Depending upon the situation, the supervisor may elect to give the employee a "fourth strike," but that is not necessary. However, depending on the performance background of the employee and the specifics of the situation, this could be appropriate.

Why do I recommend the three strikes and you're out approach? It shows fairness on behalf of the company, and it documents multiple, clear communication procedures with the employee to correct the problems. If an employee is going to be dismissed, it is imperative for the company or association to show clear, documented communication regarding what needed to be done by the employee to possibly retain his or her job and documenting that the employee did not do this and was therefore terminated.

In terms of the total time allotted for the three strikes process, it is my recommendation that not less than 60 days be utilized for this process and not more than 120 days, unless some extenuating circumstance exists. That is, from the first meeting of the supervisor and employee regarding the performance problems, the goal is that the process can be resolved either with the employee successfully addressing the problems or termination occurring within not less than 60 days and not more than 120 days. Therefore, ninety days is often a good timeframe to facilitate the process under normal circumstances. Again, this timeframe can and should be adjusted based on the specifics of each situation. It is important to allow the employee enough time to address and correct the problem performance issues. Timeframes are always adjustable depending on the specific situation.

Some people talk about the phrase "employment at will." This means that a company can terminate an employee anytime it desires. In situations where employment at will is in force, this is true. However, the question is, how much risk does a supervisor want to take in terminating an employee, especially regarding regular performance issues based on job duties, and how does the company or association want to treat employees? What is the professional and fair approach?

When you consider these questions (and make no mistake about it—these are very important questions), it is important to utilize the three strikes and you're out process and a reasonable timeframe. Sometimes, as stated earlier, other employees or people outside of the direct supervisor/employee situation are quite willing to offer opinions about how quickly an employee should be dismissed. Be clear about this—it is not their business, and it is a mistake to allow them to influence decisions regarding individual employee performance if their information and involvement is not relevant to the situation.

More Common Sense

By the same token, it is extremely important that a supervisor be able to terminate an employee who does not meet the three strikes criteria. Terminations are part of the employment process and, unfortunately, must sometimes be carried out.

When terminating an employee, it is important when no other course of action is evident, to do so expediently. If the process has been correctly facilitated, a supervisor should not feel the need to apologize to the employee for what is happening, especially if the employee had the benefits of this process and ample opportunity to correct problems. If that is the case (and hopefully it is), it is important that the termination be carried out quickly and privately. The termination should be handled in a manner that allows for as little disruption as possible of the regular workday for other employees. Terminations often occur on a Friday at four thirty or five o'clock. While some terminations cannot and should not wait for that time, it is desirable for a termination to occur at the end of the day or immediately after hours. This can be especially important when it is anticipated the confrontation will be extremely difficult and if an office needs to be cleaned out or an employee needs to be escorted out of the building. There is professional courtesy for all in not disrupting everyone else's day by trying to conduct a termination in an office full of people at 11:00 a.m. This is also obviously less embarrassing for the employee being terminated. Privacy is always best, to the extent it can be achieved.

The next important action is the appropriate and professional communication with other employees. Up to this point, other employees should not have been part of any official communication between the employee and his or her supervisor leading up to the employee termination. However, we all know that by now, most employees (if not all) will have heard of the situation. No doubt. Often, but not always, you will find the supervisor has kept the conversations confidential, but the employee feeling under attack, justifiably or not, has most likely not kept the conversations confidential. If that is the case, then so be it, and that is on the employee. However, the supervisor must maintain a confidential approach, regardless of what other employees ask or say until the termination is completed and after that as well. This is not always easy for supervisors to do. Supervisors often come under fire, especially when the employee is talking and they are not. Still, supervisors must be professional and maintain confidentiality.

Having said that, let's review an example. Let's say Employee A is terminated on Wednesday at 4:30 p.m. In today's world of texting and social media, there is absolutely no doubt that by 4:31 p.m., Employee A will have told the entire world, or at least his or her friends, about the termination and may or may not have elected to talk fairly about the situation. This is the world we live in today. It is often very difficult for supervisors trying to correctly and professionally manage employee issues to deal with today's instant communications and employees who are driven to share everything immediately.

Knowing this, it becomes very important that as soon as possible, the supervisor release a brief statement that Employee A does not work at the company anymore. There should not be details in that communication. It is not the business of other employees why the employee left and what the circumstances were regarding that departure. Even if the employee grapevine is highly proficient, which it will be, it is important the company and the supervisors conduct themselves in a professional, confidential manner. Some employees might say this isn't fair; they want to know everything, and they believe everything should be transparent. This is certainly not the case with personnel issues such as a termination. The privacy aspect is not only the correct approach for the company but also fair to the employee.

Terminations are delicate and can be difficult. Hopefully, this chapter has offered some ideas regarding fundamental approaches to deal with performance problems that may lead to a termination and how a termination may be completed through the correct process. There are always exceptions to every process, depending upon the unique nature of each personnel situation. These aspects will always be relevant and must be considered, as each situation is vitally important and unique. Personnel situations, without question, can be the most difficult situations a supervisor and an employee can face. Still, if supervisors and employees are fair, communicate well, and follow correct procedures, a situation can be handled in the best professional manner possible for all parties. Once again, the fundamental key to success on many levels is clear and proper communications.

Chapter 7

Evaluating Attitude

Is it difficult to evaluate attitude? More than that, is it appropriate? The answer—*yes* on both counts.

One of the most difficult tasks supervisors face in the performance-review process and daily supervision of employees is evaluating attitude. Certainly, not every employee is going to be extremely happy and act like sunshine every day. The reality of human nature is that it doesn't work like that for any of us. Having said that, we know it is easier for some personalities to bring a good attitude to work each day. Bringing a good attitude to work every day—meaning an attitude that is consistent, mature, positive, and grounded in reason—gives any employee a tremendous leg up when it comes to being effective, motivating employees, collaborating with other employees, and representing the company or association with the proper mind-set and image.

It can be extremely difficult for supervisors to evaluate attitude because attitude can be viewed as very subjective—but it really isn't. The outgoing individual who seems happy, talkative, and normally brings a positive attitude to work also needs to be careful to not overdo his or her positive approach—certainly not to the point of being obnoxious or wasting other employees' time.

As with all things, moderation and good judgment are very important. The gloomy Gus who comes to work every day looking only at the floor and proceeding to his or her cubicle or office without saying a word, usually has very little opportunity for a promotion or a career with longevity. This is usually not the kind of person everyone else wants to be around. Then there is the individual who always appears to be angry. I always wondered about these folks and why they were angry. I finally came to the seemingly obvious conclusion that these folks were just not happy in their jobs. Individuals who truly enjoy their job and embrace the challenges usually show it during their daily duties.

All employees need to understand that while some personalities have a leg up on bringing a positive attitude and a mature approach to work, it is a must for every employee to bring an attitude to work that is conducive to a productive workday. This is especially important for supervisors who must lead and motivate employees. We all know there will be challenging days because of company or external issues. That is just life and reality. In this chapter, I am referring to regular workdays beyond those circumstances.

It is, of course, important for supervisors to train employees in logistical issues, the mechanics of duties, and other measurable functions where a specific skill set is required and can be learned. Supervisors also have an obligation to assist employees who may be having difficulty bringing a good attitude to work, but the correction of this can be, and is, vastly more challenging because it often (not always) can have a direct correlation to personality, as I have noted. It is extremely difficult for most people (I say *most* because there are always exceptions) to accept criticism. It has been my experience that you can give most people fifty compliments, and if you criticize them in one or two areas (in a professional, constructive manner), you will still encounter resentment or disappointment. That is human nature. It is the responsibility of an employee to accept criticism in a constructive and mature manner and make the adjustments necessary to prove to the supervisor that he or she can succeed and make those adjustments. Again, this can be a very difficult task for some employees.

When a supervisor works with an employee who has an attitude problem, it is always valuable to utilize examples. Evaluating attitude is often so difficult and subjective that it is incumbent upon the supervisor to utilize examples of the problems being discussed, in the hope of providing clarity of understanding. We need to realize that many employees will not want to recognize this clarity, especially on issues of criticism pertaining to attitude. Nevertheless, it is incumbent upon the supervisor to raise these issues and initiate a process to correct the problems. Attitude problems affect literally every job duty or activity an employee tries to complete. Therefore, if a supervisor wants to get through to an employee with attitude problems, it is imperative that the supervisor provide examples to the employee showing when the attitude issues caused a problem and what happened as a result of that attitude problem. Further, the supervisor must take this to the next step, explaining how a better attitude would have prevented a bad situation or resolved a specific employee performance situation.

This is usually an interesting tightrope-type situation for supervisors, because not every employee, of course, brings the same attitude to work. For example, a variety of personality types could be considered overly forceful and yet be very appropriate for the workplace if the individual uses good judgment, good employee relations, and a positive outlook. This could be especially true depending on the duties the individual is expected to carry out.

Employees with significant skill-based talent but whose poor attitude is so detrimental to collaboration with other employees will most likely fail as productive employees and may never advance. If a daily bad attitude comes to work with an individual, it will indeed overshadow the talents of that individual. Bringing a good attitude to work, being collaborative with other employees, and moving forward through the workday in a positive fashion, is incumbent upon any employee. Attitude must be discussed during the performance review process. However, far too many supervisors avoid discussions regarding attitude because it can be a very difficult subject.

Supervisors often naturally tend to concentrate more on the accomplishments of the employee from a mechanical or logistical standpoint during performance reviews. These achievements are very important, certainly. If an employee brings a great attitude to work every day and is outstanding at carrying out duties, he or she is probably achieving a total package for success.

Earlier, I made a comment that supervisors must address the subjective nature of attitude problems by utilizing examples that caused the employee and the company problems. The use of examples provides clarity and quantifies a situation for better understanding. However, there is an even more severe attitude situation supervisors absolutely must address and nip in the bud as soon as possible.

This is what I refer to as *recreational negativism*. This describes the employee who doesn't just have a bad attitude but also enjoys complaining about everything because it provides him or her with attention. Hopefully, a supervisor can work with this employee to improve performance, not only from a mechanical or logistical standpoint but also from an attitude standpoint. The employee must understand there is no advantage to acting in this manner.

The bottom line is, employees who embrace and practice recreational negativism may very well be employees who have given up on themselves. When I say "given up on themselves," I mean the employee in question probably has determined that he or she may never be promoted or be seen as a team player. Therefore, these employees see their only course of action to gain some degree of attention is to act in this manner. It is important to state that each employee has an obligation to express his or her opinion when appropriate and to do so professionally with respect for the organization and other employees. Every employee should do this in the correct manner and through proper channels. What I am referring to is the employee who just wants to make a lot of noise to see what may happen. When an employee engages in recreational negativism as described, it is imperative that examples of how this activity causes problems be cited in his or her performance-review process. It must be made clear through documentation in the performance-review process that this type of attitude cannot be allowed.

The key is the performance-review process and the fortitude, the professionalism, and the correct approach a supervisor must use in raising these issues, utilizing examples where attitude problems exist and offering corrective solutions. These are not easy discussions. Some employees will use a variety of techniques to avoid corrective action or performance-review documentation. They will use all of the approaches you would expect as defense mechanisms. This will include indicating that they are being reprimanded because they are not a "team player" or because they think differently than everyone else, or even because they are more forward thinking than everyone else. Supervisors should not be taken in by these defense mechanisms, which no doubt will surface (and probably not in the friendliest manner) during a performance review with the employee. These are simply attempts to avoid the real issue, which is that the employee needs to straighten up and fly right and present a good, or at least acceptable, attitude each day.

It is even more difficult to correct the long-term employee with a poor attitude who enjoys recreational negativism if that employee has been allowed to function in this manner for several years. It becomes exceedingly more difficult to correct problems if the employee had previous supervisors who did not document the attitude problems, ignored the problems, and gave the employee good or even excellent performance reviews. Dealing with employees of this type requires a very professional approach on the part of the supervisor. The supervisor must be prepared for difficult discussions, must have considerable fortitude of his or her own, and must not be bothered by negative comments from the employee involved. The supervisor must realize that he or she is doing the proper thing. Some employees in extremely challenging situations, such as these noted, may take further action following a dismissal, should that occur. Therefore, it is extremely important that supervisors involve their human-resources professionals and other professional staff in making sure employee performance communication has been accurate and complete regarding what must improve. The documentation of that communication, including specifics to be achieved, must be included in the performance review. Without this documentation, the supervisor will probably fail—even though he or she may be right—if challenged by a disgruntled employee.

A disgruntled employee or an employee who is allowed to engage in recreational negativism will have a negative impact on other employees. This is especially the case if the problem employee continues to get away with the inappropriate attitude and behavior. If employees, especially younger, new employees, see no corrective action for this employee, then a certain number of those new or younger employees (or perhaps experienced employees as well) may think it is acceptable to conduct themselves in the same manner. This is when the problem employee will affect other employees. Again, I am not referring to constructive criticism of employees who understand the chain of command and have the best interest of the organization or association in mind. Employees should be encouraged to professionally challenge administrative direction on occasion, ask questions, and bring their best ideas and concepts forward. This is important, and I want to stress this point. However, they must always respect the chain of command and conduct those activities professionally.

It is important to recognize and discuss performance challenges of a subjective nature that cause difficulties. Logistical and attitude-based performance problems must be clearly communicated to the employee, including how to correct these problems. The employee in question must be given reasonable time to correct these issues. Depending upon the severity of the performance problems, these issues should be discussed, reviewed, and documented at least three times before an employee dismissal might be considered.

The point is that attitude problems are just as much (or sometimes more) of a problem than the inability of an employee to function because he or she doesn't possess the proper mechanical skills. Communication is vitally important in this process, as is documentation. However, the real challenges are the requirements that the supervisor must directly address these issues with the employee and properly conduct the review process. The employee must show the maturity and professionalism to make adjustments and move forward to a successful conclusion. These are not easy tasks for a supervisor or for the employee involved. Why is that? Human nature is the main reason, but if supervisors and employees maintain a respectful and mature approach, proceed in a step-by-step manner, and communicate clearly at each step, success is possible, and the correct results can occur.

Chapter 8

Analyzing Yourself as a Supervisor

Throughout this book, I have addressed hiring procedures, terminations, performance reviews, and related subjects. As a supervisor, how do you tackle these subjects? What is your analysis of yourself as an employee? Are you interested in an individual development plan? Do you see value in an individual development plan, knowing it is not a guarantee for an employee, but rather a road map for development that may provide benefits later? Do you embrace the performance-review process and see this as a communication tool? As you analyze your approach to these important subjects, what effect do you have on others?

You have been designated a supervisor because you are an individual with leadership skills and have proven yourself to be a proficient and valuable employee. You should be a role model. As such, you have been asked by your company to promote employee development, which may include utilizing individual development plans for employees considered to have an especially bright future. It is your responsibility to complete performance appraisals in the proper manner, with correct and fair communication to employees, including documentation to facilitate the process. It is your obligation to lead by example in regard to attitude, dedication, loyalty, and a commitment to your duties. These things may sound trite in today's world, but they are not. In today's hectic world, these characteristics and leadership traits are more important than ever. These traits have always been of paramount importance.

It is your responsibility to communicate with employees in the proper manner on behalf of the company. Interestingly, this may not always mean total transparency, certainly not to the extent of violating confidentiality with other employees or confidentiality as a member of upper management. It does absolutely mean you should communicate with employees as often as possible. When this occurs, they have ownership of the mission and direction of the organization and feel like part of the organization and not apart from it. This is extremely important. "Communication is the foundation of all successful endeavors," as I have stated on many occasions. Even with today's highly advanced electronic communications and social media, it is extremely important that we communicate completely and clearly. That may mean additional details and more complete discussions. With all the advantages offered by electronic communications and social media, we sometimes do not communicate as completely as we did in the past. Brevity is great and quick, but your communication must still be clear, accurate, and understood.

Analyze yourself—analyze your communication skills. Are your communications to employees clear? Do they understand assignments? Employees want to know why they are working on something so they can be part of it, take ownership of it, and move forward with enthusiasm. Analyze yourself—are you leading in this manner? Are you practicing fair hiring practices? Are you communicating with employee candidates in the correct manner before, during, and after an interview? Are you providing orientation opportunities to new employees or just showing them to a cubicle or office? When new employees arrive, are you taking professional responsibility for these individuals, welcoming them, and providing them a proper orientation to the company and to coworkers, as well as to the facilities? The human spirit requires positive, enthusiastic reinforcement and appreciation in order to excel. Are you saying *thank you* to your employees and to leaders as often as you should when they do a great job? Never underestimate the importance of this action.

More Common Sense

Are you utilizing the three strikes and you're out philosophy pertaining to terminations? If a termination is inevitable, have you been fair to the employee, communicated correctly, and documented in the correct manner? Have you conducted yourself ethically in your supervisory activities? Analyze yourself, and remember these important aspects of being a supervisor. These efforts require your continuing best and most detailed work on behalf of the company or association and for the employees you work with and supervise. Charge!

Chapter 9

The Nature of Human Nature

Human nature, as a subject for reflection and discussion, brings forward many thoughts regarding how we as human beings function, primarily in our interaction with other human beings. In this chapter, I will discuss several characteristics of human nature, both positive and, shall we say, challenging. The old saying, "It is what it is" probably applies to this chapter and subject more than any other chapter in the book. Throughout this book, I have discussed concepts such as recreational negativism, constructive criticism, loyalty, dedication, commitment, and a variety of topics both positive and challenging pertaining to personnel management. The characteristics of human nature reveal their own amazing ability for achievement as well as challenging aspects. Human nature is, indeed, a fascinating subject, and my commentary is based on no scientific study. My comments are my own, designed to promote awareness based on years of association-management experience.

More Common Sense

It is a foregone and obvious conclusion that some or all of these traits and characteristics will always have a bearing on how individuals react to each other and handle situations. The challenge for all of us is to recognize these various factors that make us who we are and allow us as human beings to achieve unbelievable and amazing accomplishments. The capacity of human beings for invention and accomplishments through dedication, commitment, hard work, and creativity is simply incredible. The capacity of human beings to lose sight of a goal or objective because of traits or characteristics that can cause barriers can, unfortunately, be too prevalent.

None of this is new, and that is true. What I am saying is as "old as the hills away," but again, the purpose of this chapter is to cause the reader to think about these different characteristics and traits and recognize the impact these have upon discussions or work assignments between employees and supervisors. Through that recognition, it is my hope that an increased honest and productive awareness will develop, thereby allowing us all to function better together and collaborate in a more effective and productive manner. That's a big wish list because so much of the information in this chapter deals with individual attitude and personality. We are all very different in many ways and yet also similar in many ways.

Let's begin with some fundamental commentary about positive characteristics. These include drive, pride (also on the *challenging* list as well), humility, courage, loyalty, courtesy, curiosity (on the challenging list), and control (also on the challenging list). In regard to the challenging characteristics of human nature, we will consider jealousy, insecurity, criticism, curiosity, pride, control, and worry, as well as some special commentary on gossip.

Let's begin with positive characteristics, starting with accomplishment. For most of us, accomplishment or achievement is extremely important. It is in our nature to want to know our time and effort have produced something of value. Time and effort—or perhaps better put, *energy*—are among the most important possessions any human being has. When we consider volunteer membership associations and association-management work, it is extremely important to remember that volunteer leaders and members are providing the organization with the most important possessions they have, their time and energy or effort. Therefore, to our leaders, members, staff, and employees, the need to recognize accomplishment and excel at achievement or the successful conclusion of a project is paramount. This is hardwired into our human nature, to keep us productive and motivated. We should never underestimate the importance of recognizing the accomplishment of leaders, members, staff, and employees. If we don't reach our goals once in a while, we may cease to have interest in the continued effort. That's why on occasion, it is important to break down large projects into a variety of actions or segments, so accomplishments can be recognized and celebrated as we move forward toward a larger goal. Recognition is a big part of fostering continuing motivation.

Drive enables us to achieve accomplishment. Obviously, different people have different levels of drive toward achievement. We have all read books and heard speakers throughout our professional careers talk about people with type-A personalities. These people have a great amount of drive, certainly, but all personalities, to one degree or another, will have some level of drive for accomplishment if properly motivated. In the most fundamental sense, drive is a mental state which carries us forward toward achievement.

We often hear people say, when trying to motivate a group, "How badly do you want it?" In this case, the "it" is the end goal or perhaps the next step of achievement toward a greater goal. As we consider human nature, especially in the corporate and association-management sense, we must understand that drive and determination count for a lot. An employee who is driven to expend energy, talent, and effort toward accomplishment and who understands the chain of command, as well as loyalty to the organization, is extremely valuable. That employee will overcome deficiencies in skill sets because of these factors and because the skill sets can be learned. The employee needs to understand that his or her drive must be contained (not held back, but contained—and there is a difference) within the corporate policies and reporting structure of the association or company. The employee who can do this will most likely provide great service to the company in the proper, positive manner.

Pride is another characteristic of human nature that can be amazingly complex. Most of us really desire to take pride in our work. This means fundamentally that we want to do a good job and be recognized. Having pride in one's work is extremely important because it translates to work being conducted in a quality manner. There is a huge difference between having pride in one's work and being *prideful* about one's work. Pride is a very personal characteristic. If we allow our pride get the best of us, we can negate the energy and effort we have put into our drive for a project and also may negate, to some degree, our accomplishments. Pride means that we care about what we do, and hopefully we move forward in an ethical, organized, and correct manner toward achievement of the duties we have been assigned.

We need to remember there are few things we do totally by ourselves. While we may and should take pride in something we have accomplished, it is important to recognize with pride those other people who assisted in the effort. This may be in a team format, such as a department or division. Pride is a good thing, and it has a direct correlation to our drive and why we as human beings want to do a good job and achieve. It is important to recognize the value of pride, but as with most things, in moderation. For example, we need to take pride in recognizing people for achievements. That recognition should be appropriate for the achievement.

This leads us to recognition. It is a basic, important human desire to be recognized for something we have done. People should be correctly recognized for hard work, extra effort, and achievement. Human beings move forward toward accomplishment, in many cases, depending upon the personality of the individual, often because of recognition. This means different things to different people. Some people want to be recognized and applauded, and in many cases, they should be, while other people desire to be recognized quietly. The fact remains that while different people desire recognition in different ways, it is important to understand that recognition is important to everyone. Nothing is more disheartening than to do a great job and not be recognized. That recognition may take the form of a thank-you note from a supervisor or a presentation in front of two thousand people, depending upon the situation.

Even if an individual indicates that he or she desires no recognition, there is still value in making sure that person is recognized properly, depending upon what the recognition is for. By the same token, to have value, recognition must only be given when deserved. This correctly holds up the efforts of the individual being recognized as an example for other employees or leaders.

Appropriately, following these comments on recognition are comments on humility. This can be a very difficult characteristic to discuss. Humility is a very personal reaction to recognition. To be obnoxious about achievements is not received well by other people and certainly not something that will advance your career. However, being humble to the point of embarrassing doesn't help either. The proper approach to humility is an approach that allows the individual being recognized to accept the praise or recognition in a manner that says to supervisory staff and other employees, "I notice you are recognizing me, and I greatly appreciate it. It means a lot to me, and I want to thank you." In other words, humility, correctly utilized, requires the individual being recognized to accept the recognition and be thankful in a professional and mature manner.

Another aspect of proper, humble reactions and the correct approach is, once again, the recognition of others who contributed to your success. It is a proper act of your recognition and humility to thank those who contributed to the success you have been recognized for as that is occurring. Human beings often struggle with humility. If you are overly humble, this may not come across well, and if you are arrogant or boastful in your acceptance of recognition, obviously this will be detrimental. It is important that the individual being recognized or praised not discount the recognition, as long as the recognition is appropriate. To do so negates the recognition you are receiving and does not send a good message to those providing you with the recognition or to other employees or leaders.

In other words, upon receiving praise or recognition, it is not proper action to simply shuffle your feet and say, "Aw, shucks, I really didn't do anything." It is the correct response to show appreciation in a professional manner and recognize any other individuals who also contributed to the success. Acceptance of recognition should not be long and drawn out, but it should be sincere. You should accept praise and be proud of your accomplishments with your head up and in a manner that sends a message to other employees that you really do appreciate the recognition. Humility, as with all characteristics or traits, varies to a huge degree depending upon the personality of the individual. The individual receiving the recognition should act in a tastefully humble manner and accept the recognition in a professional, businesslike manner.

Courage is another characteristic or trait that can be misunderstood. What does courage mean in an association-management or corporate environment? Let's start with what it *doesn't* mean. It doesn't mean that you proceed on your own, without permission, to move forward with some sort of work activity, program, or project. Courage means moving forward boldly to bring forward ideas and concepts for correct consideration. The key to doing this successfully is the phrase, "for correct consideration." A good employee will exhibit courage, within company policy lines and supervisory lines, to bring forward new ideas or concepts to his or her supervisor. The key for the employee bringing forth the new information is not to feel slighted or upset, should his or her ideas not be accepted. It's business; it's not personal. Many people get confused by this, and that confusion can cause problems. It takes courage to bring forward a new idea, and this should always be encouraged. We always want everyone's best ideas.

In a specific example, it takes real professional courage for both an employee and supervisor to conduct a performance review properly. Not only does it take courage to do this correctly, but it takes great maturity as well. Courage, in association management, may mean developing a new program idea and having the courage to bring it forward. It may mean, as a supervisor, having the courage to stand behind your employees when they are right and also reprimanding them when they are wrong. It means having strength of personality in carrying out your duties correctly. It means not yielding or compromising an ethical position to gain popularity. Courage may be one of the more difficult traits we encounter in wrestling with our own human nature. I believe you can have courage and certainly not violate any chain of command or company policy if you act correctly, ethically, and within that chain of command.

Loyalty is another characteristic of human nature that sometimes gets lost because of human interaction and a desire to be accepted. Loyalty includes being loyal to your supervisor and your organization, association, or company. Loyalty means you will represent the company and those you report to professionally. It means you will not allow them to be blindsided by issues that affect your work or theirs. People who don't want to be loyal are sometimes more interested in popularity or maintaining an approach that allows them to stay connected to the gossip that occurs in every company or association environment. There is a huge difference between loyalty being correctly or incorrectly implemented.

Loyalty, in many instances, simply means an employee always has the very best interest of the organization at heart and will be loyal to that interest, as long as there are no extenuating circumstances. Loyalty and dedication, and perhaps drive, may be the most important characteristics that any employee can bring to his or her work. Supervisors and companies need loyal employees with mature and professional attitudes in order to be successful. Sometimes, employees who are not correctly motivated make fun of a loyal employee. Employees who make fun of someone else for being a team player are most likely employing a defense mechanism because, for some reason, they have not achieved that status or possibly have other deficiencies that may keep them from being seen in the same capacity.

Being a team player in the correct manner is a huge compliment. What could possibly be better than being seen as a team player who contributes to the success of achieving the mission of the company or organization? One of the fundamental characteristics of these people is loyalty. Loyalty is based, first and foremost, on trust. Are you an employee your supervisor and the company can trust? Do you hold the confidence of information? Do you move forward and complete assignments on time? The list goes on and on, but you get the picture. Loyalty is an important characteristic of human nature and one that should be absolutely necessary for any employee to be promoted and to enjoy sincerely his or her duties each day.

Another aspect of human nature is courtesy. I don't need to dwell on this, because the word really is self-defining. Does this mean lying down and getting run over by everyone? Of course not. It simply means there is value to being professionally courteous. There is no value to yelling or screaming at someone. If you disagree with someone, tell that person, and this can certainly be done in a courteous, professional manner. Courtesy has to do with how we conduct ourselves. Simple acts such as thanking people or showing appreciation, which we have discussed, are important. Daily courtesy will transform into respect for you, as long as it is correctly administered. As with all things, professionalism and moderation are required. Of course, good judgment is always required.

More Common Sense

The next area of commentary has to do with curiosity, and like some other human characteristics, curiosity is on the list of both positive and challenging characteristics of human nature. Curiosity can lead us down the wrong path, possibly being interested in gossip or in someone else's business. Curiosity can lead us to desire information that may not affect us. For example, if something is happening in another department of your association or company and it has no effect on you whatsoever, then curiosity will probably not be your friend. If you have a professional relationship with your supervisor, you should be able to ask and see what type of response you get. Certainly, you should not allow curiosity alone, as a negative aspect of human nature, to move you forward to put your nose into areas where it does not belong. As we all know, people can sometimes struggle with this. It is a big mistake to take action in this manner.

By the same token, curiosity is very important to us as human beings. Where would we be without our curiosity to explore, create new projects, or develop new programs, activities, or business ventures? We would be in a sorry state without utilizing our natural curiosity to drive those efforts. Where would we be without curiosity when it comes to new inventions or medicines? Curiosity is an amazing human trait because it has the ability to drive us down a path toward great success—or if we are not careful, a path that can cause us problems in our professional career and interaction with other employees and leaders. We must focus on the positive aspects of curiosity to move forward with drive toward accomplishment.

Control is another very interesting human characteristic. All of us want to be in control of what we are doing all the time. That is basic human nature. There is great value in that control, because it is the foundation of our independent nature, which makes us productive and drives us toward achievement. Having said that, control can also cause problems, when trying to collaborate with other employees or lead a team. It can cause problems if we don't share control on occasion to foster productive collaboration. I always found it interesting to hear someone say, "He is a control freak." How many times have we heard that? To those who say this on a regular basis, I have a newsflash: everybody is a control freak. As a matter of fact, the person saying that might be just as much or more of a control freak as anyone else. All this means is that everybody wants to control what they do and how they do it. We all have different ways we want to approach our duties, how we do things in our daily lives, or conduct our own business. This is not a bad thing, but the real truth is that everybody is a control freak to one degree or another.

I don't like the word *freak* anyway, because desire for control is basic human nature. Naturally, we all want to control our own actions, destiny, and decisions. Sometimes people get confused about control and the decision-making process. Sometimes decisions are clear and who controls those decisions is indisputable. Other decisions can be based on our opinions. Certainly, a decision to do something illegal, as opposed to a decision not to conduct oneself in that manner, should usually be clear. A lot of decisions and control issues are based on opinion. Human beings, as we know, have no shortage of opinions. The way we manage control issues in a professional or business environment is by utilizing good judgment, proper ethics of conducting business issues, remembering the proper chain of command, and embracing collaboration. Those various approaches are the gatekeepers to managing control issues. Without them, we can have problems with human dynamics and moving forward in a productive manner.

Control issues can be amazingly complex. As a supervisor, I want an employee leading a department to have control, but I also don't want that employee to stymie the creativity of his or her team. I want that employee to lead the team, bring them together collaboratively, finding their best creativity and work. I want that employee to make sure the team understands their goal and to bring out the best in each team member. As with so many things in human nature, there is a tightrope to walk, and good judgment is necessary. Great judgment, ethical judgment, and judgment grounded in common sense, are paramount as we deal with all aspects of human nature and our duties. Sound judgment based on common sense, company policy, and the chain of command is so important that it cannot be stated enough. I want employees who aspire to more control, meaning employees who want to be promoted or want to put more of themselves and their ideas into the organization or association. I do not want employees who are insubordinate in their activities, taking only their own desire for control into consideration. No company desires these employees because these employees can undermine the productivity and collaboration of the entire employee group.

Let's be clear about one thing (even if you take nothing else away from this commentary): we all want control. It's hardwired into us. It may be in varying degrees, but it's just basic human nature. We need to recognize that factor, as we recognize all other factors of human nature, and as we work with employees and leaders. We need to recognize that control issues are not a bad thing if, like every other human characteristic, they are managed correctly, ethically, and professionally. Control speaks to our very independence, and this is an extremely valuable trait. I don't want to negate that point. We need to recognize that control is inherent in the personality of every human being wanting control of his or her own destiny and decisions.

Remember, I am discussing these issues as they pertain directly to a corporate or association-management environment. I am not discussing these issues as they pertain to control of one's personal life, which obviously is up to each individual. Having control is something we and many generations before us worked very hard for and sacrificed for in this country, and we should all have great pride in that. Simply put, just remember we are all control freaks,

More Common Sense

but we need to work together. Sometimes that means compromise and collaboration, utilizing good and fair judgment.

What do we do about worry? This is a big one. We all worry, worry, worry. Some of us worry more than others. This is a human characteristic we are not going to resolve, but again, we can recognize this and work with it. Human beings worry about everything. In the workplace, the challenge is to try to manage worry and stay focused on issues we are responsible for and not worry about issues others are responsible for. Sometimes we need to have faith that others will handle their affairs correctly and be held accountable. You have probably heard, "If it's not in your area or doesn't involve you, don't worry about it." This is easier said than done for most of us, thanks to our friend, human nature.

Worry can cause a variety of problems. First of all, it will increase stress, and we all have enough of that. It can cause actions, on occasion, that we would not normally consider. Like all human characteristics, worry varies a great deal, depending upon the personality of the individual. Someone who is highly motivated and who feels great responsibility for anything he or she is given to do is going to worry, most likely, more than someone who does not have those traits. Generally speaking, from a business standpoint, the higher up the management ladder you go, the more you have to worry about. People don't always recognize that about upper management, but there are more things to worry about and there are more duties to oversee. Therefore, the level of responsibility is greater. This is absolutely not to diminish the important role that every employee plays in the company or association.

So, what do we do about this? As with all things, we do our best to recognize it and deal with it. We cannot eliminate worry. I doubt that anyone has ever been successful at that. I'm not sure we would want to eliminate worry, because to a degree, worry drives us to care and take precautions and double-check our work, which has merit. The challenge with worrying is to try to manage it, so it doesn't become all-consuming or drive us down the wrong path. The way to do this is to clearly identify what we are worrying about and determine accurately what we do or do not control. Often, we need the help of others to do this, and there is nothing wrong with that. You may have a great employee who is having difficulty in an area, and you find out, as the supervisor, that the employee is worried about something. This is effecting his or her daily efforts. You might find you can put the employee's mind at ease with some information, counseling, or just a good open discussion. Often, employees are worried about something, and they don't have all the facts. Clarification can be a great help in this regard.

This is why gossip is very dangerous. Gossip can lead to increased worry, and more worry leads to additional stress. This is why the professional relationship between a supervisor and an employee, and trust in that relationship, as well as loyalty on both sides, is very important. When these factors are in place, there is an opportunity to address issues effectively that people are worried about and perhaps to eliminate some of that worry. Those are the mechanisms we have in place to help lessen worry and try to manage it to a certain degree.

As with all characteristics of human nature, worry is amazingly complex, but we need to recognize in our daily business ventures that it does exist. This is especially true when there is a corporate change, a restructuring, or anything that might involve change. Few things drive humans to worry more than change. Let's be clear about this—worrying about change is a human trait no one is going to eliminate, and it often has validity, but if there is nothing you can do about the change that is occurring, worrying about it will most likely only make your situation worse. In other words, as we discuss the nature of worry in this chapter, we need to talk about managing feelings in the right way in the business environment. This includes communicating with people as appropriate and having the trust between a supervisor and an employee to discuss what could be bothering an employee. The employee may find out there is nothing to worry about because of misinformation. The combatants to worry are communication, trust, and loyalty, as well as an acceptance of what we can and cannot control.

Let's move on to criticism. Progress needs to be made to address criticism in a mature and organized fashion and to facilitate productive discussion between the employee and supervisor. It takes courage to deliver constructive criticism and a great foundation between the supervisor and the employee, consisting of loyalty, trust, and respect to hold that discussion successfully.

Then, that discussion must include ways to address the criticism correctly and solve whatever problems exist. The supervisor, unless extenuating circumstances exist, must make it clear to the employee that he or she wants to help the employee solve problems expediently. No one likes to be criticized, and our natural human reaction to criticism is defense. The first thing any of us do when we are criticized is throw up our defenses. We want more information immediately and we often feel offended by the criticism. This is not news to anyone and is just normal human behavior. The question then becomes, "How do we proceed productively to solve the problem, move forward, and preserve or hopefully even strengthen the supervisor/employee relationship?" We do that through the use of examples and through communication, which again is the foundation of all successful endeavors. Communication is very important, as is documentation and effective and professional work between a supervisor and employee to achieve progress.

The last area I will discuss in this chapter is jealousy. Jealousy is another characteristic of human nature that has been around forever, and to some degree is unavoidable. As with almost every characteristic, jealousy is different for a wide variety of personalities. I know people who never seem to be jealous. If someone else succeeds, they are genuinely happy for that person, and glad to see him or her succeed. They join in applauding the individual. This might be a promotion at work, getting a better car, a better house, or winning the lottery, for that matter. However, quite often, these types of achievements can bother some people and can cause problems in employee relations. Jealousy can be one of the most difficult human characteristics to deal with, but it is very recognizable. It is certainly clearly recognizable by those other than the individual who is jealous. It takes a great deal of maturity and effort for the jealous person to privately recognize and deal with his or her own feelings.

For supervisors working with employees, they will often encounter jealousy when one employee is promoted over another. That's when a supervisor must be proficient in communication and counseling. Perhaps the jealous employee will have an opportunity for a promotion again in the future, but once again, there must be trust and loyalty between the supervisor and the employee to hold a conversation such as that. The jealous employee must be made aware that the jealousy is noticeable and can be self-consuming if the employee is not careful. I have witnessed conversations with jealous employees in which they have successfully recognized the problem, addressed it, communicated well, and the employee was still unable to adjust the feelings of jealousy. Sometimes the jealous employee changes positions or even leaves the company. Those actions may be the only visible answer if the situation becomes critical from a performance aspect. Hopefully, this will not be the case, and an employee will be able to recognize, following consultation with his or her supervisor, that these actions are noticeable, and there is no need to be jealous, which may be self-destructive for the employee.

It takes courage for supervisors to raise this issue. It is probably best accomplished when the supervisor lets the employee talk first, asking the employee what may be bothering him or her. As always, listening is important. It will become obvious that the jealous employee is not performing up to his or her expectations, and this may be the reason why. In other words, problems with jealousy must be brought into the open in a private discussion, and the supervisor and employee must talk about how to eliminate the effects of jealousy on day-to-day work activities.

Chapter 10

Author's Summary

The title of this book is *More Common Sense*. It is a follow-up to my first publication, *Just Common Sense*. This book deals specifically with a variety of personnel subjects as they pertain to business and more directly to association management. All of the characteristics of human nature we have discussed in this section can be addressed—whether it be problems or success stories—through communication. Once again, good communication is the crux of all successful activities in one form or another. For communication to be successful, there must be respect between a supervisor and an employee or other employees and a genuine desire on the part of all involved to succeed. This requires great maturity. That is fundamental, whether the discussion is about the implementation of an individual development plan for an especially gifted employee or dealing with any of the aspects of the nature of human nature.

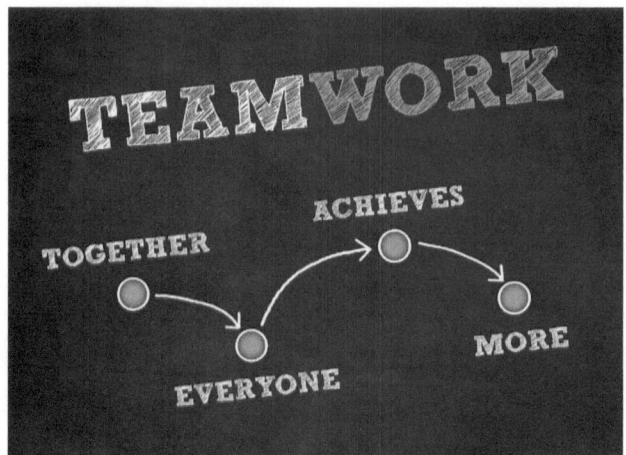

There are no secret answers to the subjects in this book because regardless of any subject, it takes work, fortitude, and communication to be successful. The purpose of the book is simply to raise awareness about all the subjects covered in the various chapters. Let us be aware and always strive to do better. As supervisors work with employees or employees work together, we all need to be aware of the various aspects of human nature and how they affect who we are and how we function.

I hope the book has stimulated your thought process in many subject areas and caused you to rethink how you conduct your day-to-day activities as a supervisor or an employee. If the book has done that, it has achieved its objective. I leave you with this: human beings are amazing, and our capacity for tremendous achievement has always been and continues to be fantastic. Let's avoid the relatively small challenges that can slow progress and productivity. We can accomplish anything we set our minds to, and that must always be foremost in our thoughts and actions. As in the past, the achievements that await us in the future will be amazing, as long as we move forward in a positive, collaborative fashion. May we always embrace that.

About the Author

Mark E. Frels, CAE, Ret. was born and raised on a multigenerational family grain and livestock farm near Hillsdale, Illinois, in upper Rock Island County. He is an honors graduate of Iowa Wesleyan University. During two summer programs, he studied language and culture at the University of Madrid, Spain. Mark began his professional association-management career with the Illinois Farm Bureau as a county Farm Bureau manager trainee in 1977. That same year, he was hired as the Knox County Farm Bureau manager, a position he held for approximately ten years. He was named Illinois Farm Bureau regional manager in 1986, covering Regions 1A and 1B, comprising thirty-six counties in the northern third of Illinois. In 1993, he was named Illinois Farm Bureau director of field services, taking his management abilities to the Illinois Farm Bureau headquarters in Bloomington, Illinois, to lead that division. Following that appointment, he was named executive director of member services and public relations and a member of the Illinois Farm Bureau management team, reporting directly to the president of the organization.

The Illinois Farm Bureau (corporate name: Illinois Agricultural Association) is the largest volunteer membership association of farmers and those supporting agriculture in the state of Illinois, with well over 400,000 members. In addition, the Illinois Farm

Bureau is one of the largest state farm bureaus in the country. Throughout his career, Mark worked with farmers and leaders at the grassroots level and was responsible for a wide variety of personnel and human-resources functions and programs, including membership acquisition and maintenance, training and development, Agriculture in the Classroom, the regional manager program, the county Farm Bureau manager program, the Rural Illinois Medical Student Loan Program, the annual convention of the association, the county Farm Bureau manager-trainee program, the arrangements for the state association to participate in the national American Farm Bureau Federation convention, and a number of other functions and administrative activities, including personnel administration and budgeting.

Mark is a certified association executive, achieving that designation from the American Society of Association Executives (ASAE) in 1986. Mark retired in 2013. He and his wife, Ann, a retired high school English teacher and retired municipal employee for the town of Normal, Illinois, now reside in rural Wyanet, Illinois.

www.ingramcontent.com/pod-product-compliance
Lightning Source LLC
Chambersburg PA
CBHW030851180526
45163CB00004B/1531